OVER BOSTON

OVER BOSTON

Aerial Photographs by David King Gleason

Foreword by Robert Campbell

LOUISIANA STATE UNIVERSITY PRESS

BATON ROUGE AND LONDON

To the two women whose support and
dedication made this book possible

Josie, *my wife, and*

Gisela, *my studio manager*

Copyright © 1985 by Louisiana State University Press
All rights reserved
Manufactured in Japan

Designer: Joanna V. Hill
Typeface: Linotron Trump Medieval
Typesetter: Moran Colorgraphic
Printer and binder: Toppan Printing Company

LIBRARY OF CONGRESS CATALOGING IN PUBLICATION DATA
Gleason, David K.
  Over Boston.
  Includes index.
  1. Boston (Mass.)—Area photographs.   I. Title.
F73.37G55 1985   917.44'61'00222   85-16633

ISBN 0-8071-1283-6

The author extends his special thanks to several individuals and companies: architects Robert Campbell and John McConnell, both of whom practice in Boston; architects Karen Dominguez (who made her library on Boston available) and John Burke, both of whom were educated in Cambridge and practice and teach architecture in Louisiana; TMA Helicopters, especially Harold Cail, Frances Flaherty, and pilots David Veazey, David Hale, Bruce MacLeod, Paul O'Meara, Richard Theriault, Albert Wilkens, Arthur Godjikian, Lance Patten, and Charles Milan; Shaughnessy Cranes for the motor crane, which was operated by John Duff; Boston police officer Stanley Saymanski, who moved us through the heavy traffic of the Hub with unfailing patience and good humor; and finally, the staff of Gleason Photography, who managed to keep the studio on an even keel in spite of my preoccupation with Boston: Gisela O'Brien, who made all the reproduction-grade color prints for this book, Josie Gleason, Craig Saucier, and Mary Ewing.

CONTENTS

Within the City

1. Long Wharf
2. Old North Church
3. Massachusetts General Hospital
4. State House
5. *Beaver II*
6. New England Aquarium
7. Old State House
8. Faneuil Hall
9. City Hall
10. Boston Garden
11. Public Garden
12. Copley Square
13. Prudential Center
14. Christian Science Center
15. Museum of Fine Arts
16. Northeastern University
17. Fenway Park
18. First Church of Roxbury
19. Fort Hill
20. Dorchester Heights
21. Charlestown Navy Yard
22. Science Park
23. Longfellow House
24. Bunker Hill Monument

In the Vicinity of Boston

1. Old North Bridge
2. Walden Pond
3. Codman House
4. Blue Hills Reservation
5. Adams Family Home
6. John F. Kennedy Library
7. Hammond Castle

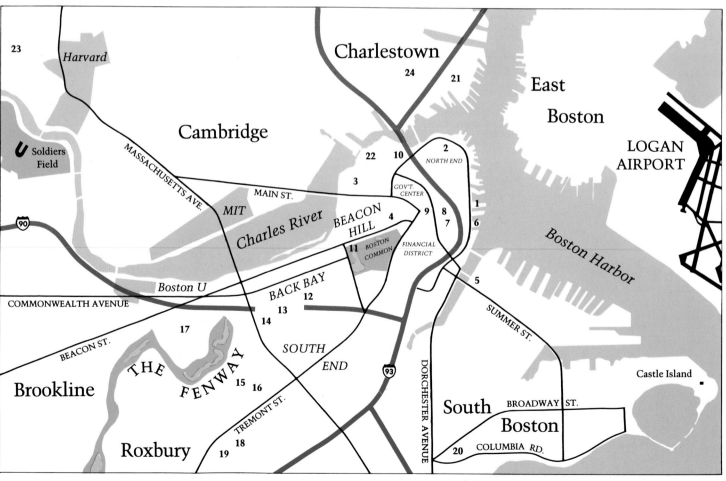

FOREWORD

by Robert Campbell

Reflecting on Boston, one thinks not of individual buildings so much as of larger, more collective chunks of cityscape—streets, parks, waterfronts, whole neighborhoods. One thinks of Marlborough Street, with its blocks of exquisite town houses; of Commonwealth Avenue, that Parisian boulevard lined with trees and statues; of Mount Vernon Street and Charles Street and Louisburg Square on Beacon Hill; of Union Park in the South End; or of the curving, rising banks of three-deckers in Dorchester. There is the Emerald Necklace, the ring of parks that tenuously touch, like dancers holding hands in a circle, as they connect the Boston Common all the way around through the city to Franklin Park. There is Harvard Square, a sleepy college crossroads as recently as the 1950s, which has now boomed into a regional commercial center without losing either its sense of place or its character, thanks to the efforts of the citizens of Cambridge, who hold every developer accountable. One thinks also of the long, serrated row of waterfront warehouses of Boston Harbor, most of them converted, since 1970, into expensive condominium apartments.

If cities were made of individual buildings, then street-level photography could tell us all we need to know about them. But cities are made, above all, of collections of buildings, buildings that join together in patterns to shape streets, squares, and quays. That is why David Gleason's photography is so valuable. It restores to us our sense that cities are continuous fabric, a weave of buildings enclosing spaces. Except for a few rare buildings that are properly monumental, the most important job any building can do in a city is not display itself but rather join in the society of buildings around a square or along a street, shaping outdoor space for human beings to inhabit. A good city is a city of outdoor rooms, of streets and squares that are like the corridors and rooms of a house, through which we move as we enact the drama of civic life. As we walk down a good street, the buildings seem to pull themselves to attention like troops on parade, troops we seem to be reviewing as we march between them. Or to change the metaphor, the building fronts seem to be the handsome paneled walls of the street space. Both metaphors—street as room, building as person—should occur to us in a good city.

Flying low over Boston in his helicopter, David Gleason, a stranger to the city, has seen and revealed this connectedness. It is a valuable lesson for all of us, because it is just this connectedness that the American city has been losing in the years since 1945, as more and more of the old built fabric is ripped apart to make room for the automobile and its insatiable desire for more and more expressways and parking lots.

Boston avoided such a fate for a curious reason: its long economic dark age, which lasted from the 1920s through the 1950s. Boston lost its first economy, shipping, to New York in the nineteenth century, then its second, leather and textiles, to other parts of the country in the twentieth. From the late 1920s through the late 1950s virtually no new buildings were built in Boston—which meant that few old ones were demolished. As the historian Lewis Mumford said in 1957: "If Boston had been prosperous, Boston would have been uninhabitable by this time. There is no reason for trying to catch up with other cities by repeating their mistakes. A few more expressways leading into Boston will turn downtown Boston into a second-rate shopping center."

It was a lesson Boston took to heart. By the 1960s it began to become clear that Boston was not dead after all. It may have been the first major city to lose its industrial base, but it was also the first to move into a postindustrial economy. As it became clearer and clearer that the next generation of Americans would be one of number crunchers and word processors, not manufacturers or laborers, Boston began to look more like a city of the future than a city of the past. Office towers sprouted downtown. Hospitals and universities expanded. Computer research, much of it spun off from the many universities, began to fill up new buildings being built along Route 128, the bypass around the city. Route 128 could have been the death of Boston, sucking economic life away into the suburbs, but things turned out the other way. The high-tech businesses on 128 needed many services—lawyers, bankers, brokers, architects, and developers. And these people by and large chose to stay downtown—near one another, near state and city government, and, perhaps most important, near the airport. Boston's airport is in its harbor, a magnificent fact that has kept the port, and therefore the business center, in the same place it always was. The only change has been from trains and ships to airplanes.

In the 1970s and 1980s, central Boston underwent a true renaissance, sparked off by the economic boom. The old Back Bay neighborhood, perhaps the finest example anywhere of nineteenth-century American city planning, was a semislum of students and transients in 1970, with less than 1 per cent of its dwelling units occupied by their owners. By 1985 the neighborhood had turned into an area of expensive condominiums and shops, with an extremely vital street life. Few were hurt by the reversal of fortunes in the Back Bay, but other parts of the city were not so lucky, as one neighborhood after another began the process of gentrification. In the North End and the South End, and to some extent in Dorchester, Cambridge, and other areas, the conflict between relatively poor, indigenous populations and newly arrived elites became harsh. The best one can say for such conflicts is that at least they are better than the long decline they replaced. And there are still many ungentrified neighborhoods, invisible to the tourist, where the families of the workers cast adrift by the departure of the industrial economy continue to subsist without participation in the boom that has enveloped the rest of the city.

But on the whole, it is the boom that characterizes recent years. The Faneuil Hall Marketplace opened in 1975. Even as late as then, there was little faith in Boston. No Boston bank would finance so risky a venture. The marketplace managed to open anyway, quickly began to draw more visitors than Disneyland, became the most profitable shopping center in the United States, and helped spike pessimism about the city's viability. At one time the markets had been threatened with possible demolition. As Mumford suggested, it was perhaps the result of Boston's being so long unsuccessful that they survived.

By the time the boom came, the preservation movement was well in place in Boston, as it was in other cities. But unlike so many other cities, Boston never tore down the old city to make a new one. It fitted the new city into the old, often with much controversy and conflict. Everyone's consciousness of urban design was raised as a result of long battles in the 1970s and 1980s over controversial development proposals. The end result was an aroused and skillful citizenry, as ready to go to war against overblown development as its ancestry had been to go to war over liberty. The preservationists do not win all the battles, but it is to the preservation movement more than to any other force that Boston owes its sur-

vival as a livable and beautiful city. The urgent need in the city today is to write laws to control development, rather than continue to let each new development proposal turn into a free-for-all.

What is the Boston we all care about so much that we want to preserve it? First, it is a red city, or at least a pinkish one, made of brick and stone in a palette that runs from orange-red to brown-gray. There are many exceptions to this rule, of course, but one of the things David Gleason's photographs confirm is the general redness of the central part of the city—of Beacon Hill, Back Bay, Bay Village, and the South End. Boston is a brick city, by and large, with considerable amounts of granite thrown in. The red coloration helps keep it looking healthy in its typically death-gray Januaries. What is not made of some kind of warm-toned masonry is likely to be wood clapboard, and the clapboard gives a ruled surface that, like brick, keeps its texture regardless of sun or shade. Concrete, on the other hand, a material much beloved by modern architects, who always seem to imagine their buildings under a Mediterranean sun, does not look good in Boston. It looks clammy and gray and makes one wish to move to California. Cities have their natural coloration; as Boston is red, so San Francisco, for instance, in its ideal manifestation, is a white city in a mist. Both should remain what they are and avoid the worldwide collapse into homogenization.

Second, Boston, as noted, is a city of collective places. It has its few architectural monuments, but not many. Trinity Church, the public library, City Hall, the State House, the Old State House, Faneuil Hall, and a few others are true foreground buildings, freestanding and symbolic of major elements of the society. But most of Boston is background buildings that collect into neighborhoods. No other American city today retains such a strong sense of its individual neighborhoods. A Bostonian will tell you he is from Southie or Charlestown rather than from Boston. Perhaps the reason for the fierce identification with neighborhood is that the city is so incredibly sliced up by natural or man-made barriers of ocean, river, channel, and turnpike. Or perhaps the reason is the successive waves of immigrants that made South Boston Irish, the North End Italian, Roxbury black. The isolation of neighborhoods within the city leads to defensiveness and bigotry but also to supportive community life within the neighborhoods.

Boston is also a conservative city. It used to be said, in the nineteenth century, that Boston ladies kept their new dresses from Paris in the closet for a year before wearing them, so that they would not look too fashionable. Boston is rarely first with a new trend in culture. It leaves the testing stage of any idea to Los Angeles and New York. Its physical form, as a result, is slow to change. What is called postmodern architecture, for instance, long the rage in New York, is only just now beginning to make an appearance in Boston. The conservatism means that everything that Boston has ever been, architecturally, is essentially still present in it, so that the city is a museum of its own past, in which cultural memory is visible. It is this presence of the past that, more than anything else, has made Boston in recent years a mecca for tourists. People call Boston a European city, but that is not really true. Instead, it is an older American city that has kept itself what it was, rather than jumping too enthusiastically into change.

Looking down from David Gleason's helicopter, you sense the slowness of change, the importance of continuity. You can also see the physical form of the city much better than you can sense it from the ground. Hating change though Boston may, the fact remains that as a geographical entity, it has changed more over its lifetime than any other American city. The skinny tadpole of the Shawmut peninsula that once stuck out into Boston Harbor with three hills on its head has evolved, through a staggering work of landfill over the centuries, into a great city. But from the air, one can still make out the form of that old peninsula and see how it has shaped the city. The so-called High Spine, for instance, that dorsal fin of skyscrapers that marches from the business district out toward Roxbury, is only a contemporary incarnation of the narrow neck of the original peninsula, which the spine closely traces. The three hills were chopped down and used to fill the coves, and when the hills were gone, more fill was brought in from the suburbs. Boston, almost as much as Leningrad or Venice, is a city made by human effort.

Along the way, there were great architects. Peter Harrison designed King's Chapel. Charles Bulfinch, the greatest architect of his day and of the so-called Federal style, designed Faneuil Hall and the "new" State House of 1797, as well as houses, churches, and University Hall at Harvard. A still greater architect appeared in the 1870s. Henry Hobson Richardson, a transplanted Louisianian, won a national competition with his design of Trinity Church in Copley Square, moved to Boston, and created the most influential American architectural practice of the nineteenth century. Among the better monuments of his burly "Richardsonian Romanesque" style in and near Boston are Trinity and its parish house, Austin Hall at the Harvard Law School, Crane Memorial Library in Quincy, and the unique Ames Gatehouse in North Easton. Richardson's firm still exists and is now the oldest in the United States and one of the largest in Boston. Now called Shepley, Bulfinch, Richardson and Abbott, it is responsible for the design of all of the Harvard houses.

Two of Richardson's draftsmen, Charles McKim and Stanford White, left the firm to form another, called McKim, Mead and White, which succeeded Richardson's as the leading American firm and designed what is possibly the city's best single work of architecture, the magnificent Boston Public Library. The library is now in process of being restored to its former glory, with the architects for the renovation being the aforementioned Shepley, Bulfinch, a fact that closes some kind of circle.

There is much fine architecture dating from the late nineteenth century but little from the early twentieth, when Boston began its sink into economic decline. There is little prairie style, arts and crafts style, or art deco in Boston. With the economic upturn a new generation of architects appeared, notably the firm of I. M. Pei and Partners, which, though headquartered in New York, has done more of its buildings in Boston than anywhere else, including the Hancock Tower by Pei partner Henry Cobb, the Christian Science Center by partner Araldo Cossutta, the John F. Kennedy Library, and a number of buildings at Massachusetts Institute of Technology, Pei's alma mater. Another important firm appeared in 1962, when two architects, neither of whom had ever done a building in his own name, won a national competition for the design of a new city hall. Gerhardt Kallmann and Michael McKinnell built their controversial city hall and went on to many other buildings, notably the American Academy of Arts and Sciences in Cambridge, a new Back Bay railroad station now under construction, and a proposed new convention center. The Architects Collaborative, Hugh Stubbins, Benjamin Thompson, the Cambridge Seven, Pietro Belluschi, Graham Gund, and Sert, Jackson are among the many architects who have made Boston and Cambridge a world capital of architecture in the past three decades. Among the better Boston buildings of these years one would have to list the MIT Chapel by Eero Saarinen, the New England Aquarium by the Cambridge Seven, the Faneuil Hall Marketplace restoration by Benjamin Thompson, Church Court condominiums by Graham Gund, Peabody Terrace apartments by Sert, Jackson, as well as the American Academy, the City Hall, and the Hancock Tower—although to name any building is to be invidious, since it means leaving out others of merit.

Styles in architecture have changed much, of course, over the years. There is little eighteenth-century architecture left in Boston, but there is a lot of fine early-nineteenth-century Federal work, with the typical flat surfaces and delicate ornament of that style. Federal was followed by Greek revival, and Greek revival by a host of other revivals throughout the later nineteenth century. The house type most people associate with Boston, the brick bowfront row house, was the dominant type in the South End, where it flourished in the 1850s, and in parts of Beacon Hill, where it dates from a few decades earlier. The so-called Boston granite style, an immensely heavy way of building that was applied to warehouses, to the navy yard, and to some downtown office buildings, was a feature of the early nineteenth century. When Richardson appeared, his work was sufficiently influential to dominate a whole generation of richly carved and modeled buildings by followers such as the firm of Peabody and Stearns. McKim, Mead and White brought in what is called American renaissance, which imitated Italian Renaissance buildings and was a more scholarly style than Richardson's. The next and last of the great premodern styles in Boston was Georgian revival, style of numerous Harvard buildings from the 1910s through the 1930s. Down the river, MIT was meanwhile going for classical revival in its great Roman-domed campus by Welles Bosworth, but classical revival was never a major Boston style elsewhere except in suburban houses.

The modern style reached Boston by way of Walter Gropius, founder of the legendary Bauhaus school in Germany, who became head of the architecture program at Harvard in 1937. It flourished in the 1950s and 1960s in the form of elegant, spare, abstract buildings. Gropius' successor at Harvard, Josep Lluis Sert, added bright color and sculpted form to local modernism. Eventually, however, the modern style's tendency to ignore both context and popular taste led to its downfall. Current Boston architecture tends rather to copy imagery from the past, for better or worse, or literally to recycle older buildings.

Boston looks beautiful in these photographs. Its restored Victorian neighborhoods shine. Its coastline of mansions and beaches on the north and south shores engages one's fantasies as it always has. Its domesticated river, the Charles, is alive with white sails. To quote Mumford once again, "The value of the city is the value of having in a small area all the possible facilities for economic and social and cultural life." Unlike other cities, Boston does remain small and close-packed. These photos show it to us in a new way and thus re-create the city by the transforming perspective of art. As another author and occasional Bostonian, Robert Frost, put it: "If you say a thing three times, it stops being true." David Gleason has found a way of saying *Boston* that has not been said before, and in doing so he has created anew the truth of the place.

PART ONE

The North End

Boston, Circa 1764

Known as the Carwitham View of Boston, this line engraving was published by Carington Bowles, Map and Printseller of London.

The cleared hill overlooking the waterfront at center left is Fort Hill, and Long Wharf is in the center. At the landward end of Long Wharf, facing the sea, is the Old State House, then called the Town House. Clark's Wharf is to the right of Long Wharf. The North End is at the right, marked by the tall spire of Christ Church, the "Old North Church." The smaller church at extreme right is Newport's Meetinghouse, later demolished. The smaller church to the left of Christ Church was the original Old North.

Between Long Wharf and Fort Hill, in the background, are Boston's famous three hills, or "trimount": Beacon Hill, Mount Vernon, and Pemberton (or Cotton) Hill. The tallest, topped by a tripodlike structure, is Beacon Hill. Between the water and Beacon Hill is King's Chapel, which has a steeple with a cock on top.

Courtesy Library of the Boston Atheneum

2

Boston at Sunrise, 1984

More than two centuries later, the Long Wharf still stands, extending into the harbor toward right center. Behind it is the North End, virtually unchanged in the last century. Toward the extreme right is the spire of the Old North Church, and at the left is the Fort Point Channel.

4

The North End

The North End was virtually an island when Boston was founded, and it became one literally when early settlers dug Mill Creek through the swamps to create a source of water power using the high tides. By 1650 the North End was accessible only by two drawbridges at North and Hanover streets. It remained an island until Mill Creek was filled in during the nineteenth century.

At left is the United States Coast Guard Station, and the North End Playground is at the right, next to the water. The white spire dominating the North End is Christ Church, the "Old North Church" where Paul Revere's signal lanterns warned of the British march to Lexington and Concord in 1775. In this view, looking southwest, Boston's historic wharves are at the left, the financial district's skyscrapers are at the right, and the Government Center is at the extreme right. In the rear is South Boston.

The Fort Point Channel and the Financial District (right)

The Fort Point Channel, separating South Boston from the central business district, is spanned by three bridges. They are, left to right, Summer Street, Congress Street, and Northern Avenue. To the left of the Summer Street Bridge, overlooking the channel, are the South Postal Annex and the Stone and Webster Building. Behind Stone and Webster is six-sided One Financial Place, forty-six stories tall, on Dewey Square. Just across Summer Street is the aluminum-covered Federal Reserve Bank of Boston. In the channel, at the Congress Street Bridge, is the Boston Tea Party ship. Beyond the Northern Avenue Bridge can be seen the Custom House tower and the twin Harbor Towers.

Bird's-Eye View of Boston, Circa 1850

Drawn on stone by C. Matter and printed by
R. Furrer, this chromolithograph was published in
New York by J. H. Locher. At this time the Back

Bay, with the exception of the Public Garden, was
still a tidal marsh. Looking toward the east, this
view has the Bunker Hill Monument at extreme
left. Across the Charles (to the right) from the monument are the North End and the waterfront. East
Boston is at upper left.

The State House and Beacon Hill are at left center. The Massachusetts General Hospital and, closer
to the Public Garden, the Charles Street Meetinghouse rest on the banks of the Charles River. On
the opposite side of the Public Garden, at lower
right, are residences (town houses) overlooking the

garden, and the yards of the Boston and Providence
Railroad.

Courtesy Library of the Boston Atheneum

The Common and the Public Garden

Looking east from above Arlington Street in the foreground, this view shows the Public Garden, lying just west of, and adjacent to, the Boston Common, itself virtually unchanged since the city was founded in 1630. On ground that was formerly salt marsh, filled in during the early 1800s, the garden was designed by architect George Meacham in 1860. At left is Beacon Hill, where the State House with its golden dome stands on what was originally the highest of Boston's three hills. On the far side of the Common is the city's financial district. In the distance toward the left are East Boston and Logan Airport, which was constructed entirely on filled land.

North End Panorama (overleaf)

The Old North Church

Christ Church, the Old North Church, has dominated the North End since its construction in 1723. Designed by William Price, bookseller, organist, and warden of the church, the church has a 190-foot steeple, which was not added until 1740. Hurricanes in 1804 and 1954 destroyed the steeple, but it was replaced both times. Today it is still capped by the original weather vane, and the tower houses the first British-cast bells in North America. The largest of the seven weighs 1,545 pounds. A guild to ring them was organized by Paul Revere.

The Blackstone Block (right)

Listed on the National Register of Historic Places, the Blackstone Block lies between Blackstone Street, in the foreground, and Congress Street, which separates it from City Hall, in the background. The winding streets of early Boston still survive in this block, and its architecture reflects three centuries. In the upper right corner of the block, at Creek Square, is the Boston Stone (1737), which marked the starting point for measurement of mileages from Boston. Toward the center of the block is the Union Oyster House (the business dates from 1826), originally the Capen House, built in the early 1700s. At left is the Bostonian Hotel, designed by Mintz Associates in 1980 to retain the old street patterns of the block. Along Blackstone Street in the foreground is the Haymarket, where vendors sell fresh fish, fruits, and vegetables on weekends.

11

Sailing in the Inner Harbor

In the summer the Inner Harbor is filled with sailboats. Many of the old wharves have been converted to condominiums, allowing their owners to dock their boats alongside.

PART TWO

*Beacon Hill and
the Central Business District*

The Charles River Basin and Back Bay

At sunrise the tower of the old John Hancock Building is reflected in the Hancock Tower on Copley Square in the Back Bay. At left is a part of the Massachusetts General Hospital complex in the West End, and in the center, the Charlesbank Playground. In the foreground is the dome of the Hayden Planetarium of the Museum of Science, which spans the Charles River. In the rear at the right is the Prudential Tower.

Massachusetts General Hospital and the Charles Street Jail (right)

Massachusetts General Hospital extends northward along Charles Street, immediately adjacent to the Charles Street (Suffolk County) Jail, designed by Gridley J. Fox Bryant in 1851 and still in use. It has been expanded twice, in 1901 and 1920, following Bryant's original design. At lower right, nestled alongside the jail's southwest wall, is Buzzy's Drive-In.

The Ether Dome

The Massachusetts General Hospital was incorporated in 1811, and seven years later, construction began. The hospital's design was awarded to Charles Bulfinch, and it proved to be his last Boston project before he left the city to become one of the architects of the United States Capitol. The one-hundred-bed facility was topped by an operating amphitheater beneath a skylighted dome, where the first public demonstration of ether as an anesthetic was carried out by Dr. John Collins Warren, one of the hospital's founders, in 1846.

Beacon Hill and the Boston Common (right)

Old as Boston itself, the fifty-acre Common, common ground on which Boston's freemen could graze their cattle, is the oldest public park in the nation. Near the center of the park on its highest elevation, Flagstaff Hill (center foreground), stands a monument to Union soldiers and sailors of the Civil War. Between the monument and Beacon Street, the Common's northern boundary, is cement-lined Frog Pond, a wading pool in the summer and an ice rink in winter.

Beacon Hill, developed primarily during the first quarter of the nineteenth century, has been essentially residential since that time. Originally called Tremont or Trimount by early colonists, the area had three hills—Cotton Hill, Beacon Hill, and Mount Vernon. Beacon Hill was the highest. Today its summit is sixty feet lower than it originally was, because early developers carted off soil and gravel from the three hills to fill in the old North Cove (near today's North Station) and the area around Charles Street. The State House, designed by Bulfinch, stands near the location of the former summit of Beacon Hill. In the background, to the north, is Charlestown; the Charles River Basin is at the left, and the Inner Harbor at the right.

Louisburg Square in Autumn

Said to be the original site of Christmas caroling in
America, Louisburg Square is distinguished by its
own private green. Adjacent property owners have
the only keys to the cast-iron fence surrounding the
park. Occupants of some of the bowfront houses
overlooking the square have included William Dean
Howells, Louisa May Alcott, and Swedish soprano
Jenny Lind, who married her pianist-conductor
in number 20.

Louisburg Square in Winter (right)

Beacon Hill from Above Louisburg Square

The Second Harrison Gray Otis House (right)

Located at 85 Mount Vernon Street on Beacon Hill, the Second Harrison Gray Otis House, designed by Charles Bulfinch in 1800, is one of the few free-standing houses on the Hill. Harrison Gray Otis was a mayor of Boston, congressman, and United States senator, as well as one of the prime developers of Beacon Hill. Bulfinch designed three houses for Otis, and this second one has been called "the most endearing."

21

Beacon Street from the State House

Beacon Street as it winds westward toward Back Bay from in front of the Massachusetts State House

The Massachusetts State House (right)

Facing Beacon Street and the Boston Common is the Massachusetts State House, designed in 1795 by Charles Bulfinch, a Boston physician's son and graduate of Harvard.

Beacon Hill

Looking north toward Chestnut Street on Beacon Hill

The State House (right)

The State House, built of red brick, was completed in 1797. The rear annex, by Charles E. Brigham, was added in 1895, and the two marble wings, by Chapman, Sturgis and Andrews, in 1917. Originally, the dome of the State House was covered with whitewashed shingles, which were replaced with copper by Paul Revere and Sons in 1802. It was covered with gold leaf in 1861 and has remained golden except during World War II, when it was painted gray.

The Eastern End of the Common

The white steeple at the center, just downhill from the State House, is that of Park Street Church, located at the intersection of Park and Tremont streets. A large granary occupied the site until 1809, when it was removed (the sails of the USS *Constitution* were made in its loft). Park Street Church was built shortly afterward, following a design by Peter Banner. The green space to the left of the church is the Old Granary Burial Ground, which contains the graves of John Hancock, Samuel Adams, Paul Revere, and the victims of the Boston Massacre.

Park Street Church faces Tremont Street. The first intersecting street to the right along Tremont is Winter Street, which begins a pedestrian mall leading to Downtown Crossing, one block to the rear, where Filene's and Jordan Marsh, two of Boston's oldest and best-known department stores, are located along Washington Street, which parallels Tremont.

At the intersection of Tremont and Winter, within the boundaries of the Common, is the Park Street Subway Station, part of the nation's first subway system. To the right of the Winter Street intersection, facing the Common, is the Episcopal Cathedral Church of St. Paul (1820).

Chinatown and the Financial District (right)

The junction of the Massachusetts Turnpike and the Fitzgerald Expressway is in the foreground of this view, which looks north toward the financial district. Chinatown is at the center, to the left of the expressway, and the South Station is at the right edge.

Looking North from over Fort Point Channel (overleaf)

*The Boston Tea Party Ship and the Financial
District*

In the center of the Fort Point Channel (foreground)
at the Congress Street Bridge is the *Beaver II*, a rep-
lica of one of the Boston Tea Party ships. The
"party" actually occurred farther north, toward the
center of this picture, since the waterline was ap-
proximately where the expressway is now located.

At left rear is the facade of the South Station, and
behind it the six-sided tower of One Financial Place
(Jung, Brannen Associates, 1983). The Federal Reserve Bank of Boston (Hugh Stubbins Associates,
1977) overlooks Congress Street, dwarfing the
United Shoe Machinery Building (Parker, Thomas
and Rice, 1930), which was the tallest building in
Boston when it was built and the city's first art deco
skyscraper. To the right of the United Shoe Machinery building are the towers of the financial district, and to the extreme right is the Custom House.

*The Grain and Flour Exchange and the
Custom House Tower*

Originally headquarters for the chamber of com-
merce, the castlelike Grain and Flour Exchange
Building (Shepley, Rutan and Coolidge, 1892) is a fa-
miliar sight to motorists on the John F. Fitzgerald
Expressway near the Custom House, which in this
photograph is immediately behind it. The original
Custom House, only a corner of which can be seen
in this view, was a handsome Greek revival building designed by Ammi B. Young and completed in
1847. At the time, the water's edge was nearby.
About seventy years later, Peabody and Stearns designed the thirty-story tower to surmount the Custom House. It was completed in 1915 and for several decades was Boston's tallest structure.

The Old State House

The Old State House, seen here from Washington Street, was built in 1713 to replace the old Town House that had been destroyed in the great fire of 1711. The front faces State Street, which leads to Long Wharf. The Boston Massacre took place in 1770 in front of the Old State House, and two years later the first stagecoach to New York City left from its Washington Street entrance. On July 18, 1776, Bostonians first heard the words of the Declaration of Independence, read from the balcony.

Long Wharf (right)

Begun in 1710, Long Wharf was the centerpiece of Boston's busy harbor, and originally it extended from King Street (now State Street) near the Old State House, barely discernible between skyscrapers in the background, well out into the harbor. Land-filling in the nineteenth century and the construction of the Fitzgerald Expressway have shortened its length considerably. Packed with warehouses and shops and lined with clipper ships in its prime, Long Wharf still bears the Custom House Block, built in 1845, and the Chart House Restaurant, originally the Gardiner Building, which dates from 1763. Behind them is the Long Wharf Marriott Hotel, completed in 1982. At left, in the foreground on Central Wharf (1819), is the New England Aquarium, and at right, between Long Wharf and Commercial Wharf, is the Christopher Columbus Waterfront Park.

The New England Aquarium

At the eastern end of Central Wharf is the New England Aquarium, which houses a five-story central tank, the world's largest, of 200,000 gallons, and over seventy gallery tanks that reproduce the natural environment of their inhabitants. At right is its floating amphitheater, the *Discovery*, which rises and falls with the tides. At left is the tip of Long Wharf, and in the upper right is an excursion boat leaving the Inner Harbor for a tour of the Harbor Islands.

Commercial Wharf (right)

When Atlantic Avenue (winding about the top of this photograph) was built about 1868, it cut the great granite warehouse of Commercial Wharf in two. The warehouse was designed in 1832 by Isaiah Rogers. The section east of Atlantic Avenue, extending into the harbor, was renovated in 1968 and 1969 by Halasz and Halasz, who adapted the building for commercial and residential purposes. The western end, across Atlantic, was renovated by Anderson, Notter Associates in 1971. At the upper left is Christopher Columbus Waterfront Park, which was built in 1971 and extends between Commercial and Long wharves.

Looking South Along the Waterfront

The Pilot House, built in 1863 by the Eastern Railroad, is at lower right. Then, from bottom to top are Lewis Wharf (1836), Commercial Wharf, Columbus Waterfront Park, and Long Wharf, with its Custom House Block, Gardiner Building (now the Chart House Restaurant), and Long Wharf Marriott Hotel.

Union Wharf (right)

Farther north along the waterfront is Union Wharf, built in 1846, and restored in 1979 by Moritz, Bergmeyer. New condominiums, shown here, were added at its tip.

The Custom House District, the Financial District, and the Government Center

Looking west over the John F. Fitzgerald Expressway in the foreground, this view shows the Custom House district at left. Behind it, to the southwest, is the financial district, and in the lower center are the Faneuil Hall Marketplace and Faneuil Hall. To the rear of Faneuil Hall, at right center, are Boston's City Hall, the crescent shape of One Center Plaza, the Suffolk County Courthouse, and the State House. In the background, at right, are the Charles River Basin and Back Bay. In the center are the tallest buildings in New England, the John Hancock and Prudential towers. To their immediate left is the South End. The Blue Hills Reservation is on the horizon at extreme left.

Faneuil Hall and the Faneuil Hall Marketplace (right)

An English country market of the early eighteenth century was the inspiration for Faneuil Hall, designed by an artist named John Smibert for Peter Faneuil, who gave it to Boston for town meetings and a public market in 1742. The lower floor was left open to act as a market, and the upper floor contained a large meeting room and smaller offices for town officials. It was at Faneuil Hall, "the Cradle of Liberty," that Samuel Adams in 1772 suggested setting up the colonial committees of correspondence.

Charles Bulfinch was commissioned in 1806 to provide additional space within the hall. This he did by doubling its width and adding another story. He also moved the cupola on its roof from the center to the dockside end. As Boston grew, so did its need for additional space at the market. In 1826 Mayor Josiah Quincy presided over the construction of a granite market house, 535 feet long, designed by Alexander Parris, between Faneuil Hall and the water's edge. It was Boston's largest project up to that time.

Between 1976 and 1978, architects of Benjamin Thompson and Associates restored and recycled the historic complex for the Rouse Company, making the Faneuil Hall Marketplace a showplace of modern Boston.

Looking Toward the Sea from Faneuil Hall

The Custom House tower is at the right, and the sixteen-story, gable-roofed tower of the Marketplace Center is under construction in center background.

Boston City Hall

Based on an award-winning design by architects Kallmann, McKinnell and Knowles, Boston City Hall was built in 1968 on the site of old Scollay Square and is part of the master plan for the Government Center by I. M. Pei and Associates. The Government Center has been one of the major factors in the revitalization of the waterfront area. Within the building, the spaces most used by the public are on the ground levels, easily accessible, whereas offices not often visited by the public are on the higher floors.

The Boston Garden

The home of the Celtics of the National Basketball Association and the Bruins of the National Hockey League, the Boston Garden was built in 1928 and has a seating capacity of 15,509.

PART THREE

*From the Back Bay
to South Boston*

Boston Public Garden

Looking northwest over what once was a tidal marsh known as the Back Bay, this view has the Boston Public Garden, oldest botanical garden in the country, in the foreground, bordered at right by Charles Street. Across Charles is the western edge of the Boston Common, which met the water at about this point. Commonwealth Avenue, two hundred feet wide, begins at the left of the garden, and the Charles River Basin is in the background. Cambridge is across the river.

Swan Boats at the Public Garden (right)

Pedal-powered swan boats have delighted children and adults alike since 1877. They have been operated by the Paget family since their first voyage. At right is Thomas Ball's equestrian statue of George Washington.

Equestrian Statue of Washington in Winter

Thomas Ball's equestrian statue of George Washington (1869) in the Public Garden faces Back Bay, across the intersection of Arlington Street and Commonwealth Avenue in the upper left.

Equestrian Statue of Washington in Spring (right)

Budding magnolias are the first signs of spring along Commonwealth Avenue.

The Hatch Shell

At the left, on the Esplanade on the Charles River Basin near Beacon Hill is the Hatch Shell, since 1929 site of the Boston Pops summer concerts. Toward the center is the Public Garden, and part of Back Bay is at the right.

First and Second Church

At 60 Marlborough Street is the First and Second Church in Boston (Unitarian). First Church was incorporated in 1630, and its sanctuary was built on Back Bay in 1867. When all but the tower and rose window burned in 1968, the congregation of the Second Church (founded in 1649) combined with that of the First to form the new church, which incorporated the remains of the old structure with an entirely new, copper-roofed sanctuary in 1972. Paul Rudolph is the architect.

49

A Block in the Back Bay

Along the north side of Commonwealth Avenue, between Clarendon and Berkeley, looking toward downtown Boston in the distance. The taller building at the end of the block is eleven-story Haddon Hall, designed as a residential hotel in 1894. It caused a controversy at the time of its construction and resulted in height restrictions for Back Bay, a neighborhood said to contain the finest collection of Victorian architecture in the United States.

Commonwealth Avenue (right)

Commonwealth Avenue, which suggests a French boulevard, is the central boulevard of Back Bay. Two hundred feet wide, it has a continuous park in its middle ground, linking the Public Garden and Boston Common with the Fenway at Back Bay's western end.

51

Trinity Church

Called "one of the great monuments of American architecture," Trinity Church, completed in 1877, was designed by one of America's foremost architects, H. H. Richardson, born on a Louisiana plantation and educated at Harvard. Since the great church rests on filled land, its foundation is supported by 4,500 wooden piles, 2,000 of which, in a ninety-foot-square area, support the central tower, said to weigh eleven million pounds. Trinity is reflected in the John Hancock Tower, New England's tallest building, designed by Henry Cobb of I. M. Pei and Partners.

Boston Public Library (right)

Facing Copley Plaza from the west is the Boston Public Library, center. Opened in 1895, it was intended by the architects and the library's trustees to be "a palace for the people." The building it replaced dated from 1854 and was the country's first public library in a large city. The present library's design, by McKim, Mead and White, influenced architecture for the next forty years. At left, in the background, is the complex of hotels and offices of Prudential Center, and at right is the New Old South Church.

Copley Square

Copley Square in Back Bay became a religious and intellectual center for Boston in 1871, when the Museum of Fine Arts was built on the site of the present Copley Plaza Hotel (1912). It was followed by the New Old South Church in 1874 and Trinity Church, designed by H. H. Richardson, in 1877. The Boston Public Library came in 1895.

Starting around the square with Trinity Church at twelve o'clock and proceeding clockwise: At one o'clock is the mirror-sheathed, sixty-story John Hancock Tower; at three o'clock, the Copley Plaza Hotel. Facing Trinity on the opposite side of the square is the Boston Public Library, with its central courtyard and, away from the square, its 1972 addition. At seven o'clock is the New Old South Church.

Looking East over the Back Bay (right)

The Esplanade and Storrow Drive are at left, and paralleling them, left to right, are Beacon, Marlborough, Commonwealth in the center, Newbury, and Boylston. In the foreground, crossing Commonwealth, is Charlesgate East, at the beginning of the Fens.

Looking East from over the High Spine (overleaf)

The Museum of Fine Arts

The Museum of Fine Arts lies between the Fenway, in the background, and Huntington Avenue, in the foreground. The original building opened in 1909, and it has experienced several expansions: in 1915 and 1928, in the 1960s, and most recently in 1970. At right are some of the buildings of Northeastern University.

The Fenway (right)

Boston's "Emerald Necklace," the Fenway, was designed in 1881 by one of America's great landscape architects, Frederick Law Olmsted, who also laid out New York's Central Park and New Orleans' Audubon Park. The Fenway is part of a continuous chain of public park spaces that link the Boston Common with Franklin Park. At right is Northeastern University, and at extreme right, the Museum of Fine Arts.

A Stone Bridge, Designed by H. H. Richardson, in the Fens

Dorchester Three-Deckers (right)

In 1630 the Reverend John White encouraged a number of his parishioners in Dorsetshire, England, to settle in the New World, and this resulted in the founding of Dorchester, a fishing and shipbuilding town. Later known for its mills and pottery works, Dorchester is today primarily residential and perhaps best known for its "three-deckers"—three-family dwellings first built around Savin Hill.

61

Fort Hill

On Fort Hill in Roxbury stands a Gothic water tower topped by an observation balcony from which can be seen what were the major strategic landmarks during the seige of Boston in 1775 and 1776. The hill once stood much higher, but it was lowered after the Civil War to provide fill for Town Cove, near the Old State House along the Boston waterfront.

The First Church of Roxbury (right)

On John Eliot Square in Roxbury is the oldest wooden church building in Boston, the First Church of Roxbury (Unitarian). Built in 1804, it was the fifth structure on the site. The tower has a bell cast by Paul Revere. The congregation was founded in 1632 by John Eliot, who preached at the first two meetinghouses.

It was from this church that William Dawes departed on the night of April 18, 1775, to alarm the countryside that the British were sending troops to Concord, about twenty miles west of Boston, with orders to confiscate military supplies stockpiled by the colonists. Paul Revere, taking a shorter route, left Boston's North End that same night, going by boat to Charlestown and then by horseback to join Dawes at Lexington six miles east of Concord.

South Boston, Dorchester Heights, and Dorchester Bay

Dorchester Heights overlooks Dorchester Bay, at right, across which can be seen the John F. Kennedy Library at Columbia Point. Behind the monument on the heights is South Boston High School.

Dorchester Heights National Historic Site is a part of Boston National Historic Park, which includes the Charlestown Navy Yard, Bunker Hill Monument, Paul Revere House, Old North Church, Old State House, Old South Meetinghouse, and Faneuil Hall.

Dorchester Heights (right)

Telegraph Hill on Dorchester Heights is in the foreground. On the night of March 4, 1776, two thousand troops under the command of General John Thomas dragged cannon from Fort Ticonderoga in New York to Dorchester Heights. They brought the British occupying Boston under the range of cannon fire and forced their evacuation by St. Patrick's Day, March 17, 1776.

The Waterfront at Twilight (overleaf)

PART FOUR

*Along the Charles
and to Concord*

Bunker Hill Monument

From over Charlestown looking south toward the North End, this view shows the Bunker Hill Monument (center foreground) on Breed's Hill. In the darkness the patriots thought they were building their hurried fortifications on Bunker Hill, but when the sun rose, they found that, unfortunately, they had built on the wrong elevation, within cannon range of British batteries on Copp's Hill in the North End, just across the water.

At the right of the monument is a statue of Colonel William Preston, who, as the British troops advanced from the approximate location of the Charlestown Navy Yard at center left, told his men, "Don't fire until you see the whites of their eyes."

Old Ironsides (right)

The USS *Constitution*, the nation's oldest commissioned fighting ship, is berthed at the Charlestown Navy Yard. Built in Boston, the *Constitution*, also known as Old Ironsides, was launched in 1797. With a length of 204 feet, the 2,250-ton ship carried a crew of 475. She fought the Barbary pirates and carried fifty-two guns in the War of 1812, during which she won forty-two engagements with the British.

Charlestown Navy Yard

The navy yard, opened in the early 1800s, built warships and made rope and anchor chain for the United States Navy until after World War II, during which the yard built 141 ships. In this view, moving from top toward bottom, are the Commandant's House (1809), the Marine Barracks (1823), and the octagonal Telephone Exchange (1852). The large gray building in the foreground contains the old sail loft, and the smaller, one-story structure that approaches from lower right is the northern end of the Ropewalk (1836).

Science Park

Built on the Charles River Dam, Science Park contains the Museum of Science and the Hayden Planetarium, whose white dome is at left. The museum is the successor to Boston's Museum of Natural History, built in 1863 in the Back Bay and now occupied by Bonwit Teller Department Store.

Crossing the Charles River Basin in the rear is the Longfellow Bridge, linking Cambridge, at right, with Beacon Hill. At center left is the Charlesbank Playground, and in the left rear, overlooking Back Bay, are the John Hancock and Prudential towers.

The Great Court at Massachusetts Institute of Technology

Across the Charles from the Back Bay, where the school began in 1865 on Copley Square, is Massachusetts Institute of Technology, which moved to its new quarters in 1913. Flanked by the McLauren and Rogers buildings, which were designed by William Welles Bosworth, the Great Court defines the center of the MIT campus and faces Memorial Drive along the Charles River. Massachusetts Avenue curves off to the left.

The Green Building, Hayden Library, and Ashdown House at MIT (right)

The tallest building on the MIT campus is the Green Building, the Center for Earth Sciences, a twenty-one-story structure designed by I. M. Pei and Partners in 1962. Across the court from the Green Building is an Alexander Calder sculpture. At left, overlooking the river, is the Hayden Library. Ashdown House is at right, at the corner of Memorial Drive (foreground) and Ames Street.

Looking over MIT Toward Back Bay

Crossing the Charles is the Harvard Bridge. Massachusetts Avenue enters the picture at lower left and passes the domed, columned entrance to the McLauren Building. Directly across Massachusetts Avenue is the student union building. Toward the river from the union building is the small, circular Kresge Chapel, and across the green from it is the three-cornered dome of the Kresge Auditorium. Both were designed by Eero Saarinen in 1954 and 1955. The excellence of the auditorium's design has brought it a reputation as "the finest twentieth-century auditorium space in the Boston region."

At right, on the river, is the Baker House, designed by Alvar Aalto in 1947. Its river side undulates along Memorial Drive. The white-roofed building in the right foreground is the ice hockey rink.

Boston University at Dawn (right)

Between MIT and Harvard, but on the opposite side of the Charles River, is Boston University, located near Kenmore Square and the Fenway. Chartered in 1869, the university began as a series of small colleges. Looking eastward along the Charles River, this view has the university in the foreground. The tall building in the right foreground is the Law and Education Tower. The twin buildings in the center and right foreground in front of the tower are, on the left, the Metropolitan College and School of Theology Building and, on the right, the School of Management and College of Liberal Arts Building. Between them, set back from Commonwealth Avenue, is the Gothic-style Marsh Chapel.

Boston University

In the 1960s, following a master plan by Josep Lluis Sert, dean of Harvard's School of Design, the university expanded between the Charles and Commonwealth Avenue, erecting the George Sherman Union Building (extreme left) in 1963, the adjacent Mugar Memorial Library in 1966, and the Law and Education Tower in 1965. In the background are downtown Boston and Back Bay and, across the Charles, MIT. Entering the picture at lower left are Commonwealth Avenue and the Massachusetts Turnpike Extension.

Harvard's Graduate School of Business Administration (right)

Farther up the Charles, across the river from the main part of the campus, is Harvard's Graduate School of Business Administration, with Baker Library, crowned by the white steeple, in its center. Overlooking the river on the opposite side are the three towers of Peabody Terrace, married students' housing.

Harvard Stadium

Built in 1903, Harvard Stadium, at Soldiers' Field across the river from the campus in Cambridge, was the first collegiate athletic stadium designed for permanence and the first large reinforced-concrete building in the world. To the left of the stadium is the Harvard Athletic Facility, for indoor swimming and track. Across Harvard Avenue is the Graduate School of Business Administration.

The Weld Boathouse near the Anderson Bridge at Harvard (right)

The Harvard Yard

This view looks eastward, with the Harvard Yard, the oldest part of Harvard University, in the foreground. The yard is bordered on two sides by Massachusetts Avenue (foreground and at right) and on another side by Broadway, at left.

In the center foreground is the Johnson Gate (1889), located between two of Harvard's oldest buildings, Harvard Hall (1764) and Massachusetts Hall (1718), the oldest Harvard building still standing. Harvard and Massachusetts halls, with a third building long since demolished, formed a courtyard that faced Massachusetts Avenue. The north side of Harvard Hall faces Holden Chapel (1742), which faces the gate at lower left. Harvard Hall thus joined with Holden Chapel and with Hollis Hall (1762), on its eastern side, to create another courtyard.

Across the Old Yard, facing the Johnson Gate, is University Hall, a gray building designed in 1813 by Bulfinch, who also designed Stoughton Hall (1804), to the left of and similar to Hollis Hall.

Adjacent to and directly east of the Old Yard is the Tercentenary Quadrangle, defined by University Hall on the west side, Memorial Church (1931) at the north, Sever Hall (designed by H. H. Richardson in 1878) on the east side, and the Widener Library (1913) on the south.

The Harvard Campus

Looking south toward the Charles River, this view shows the Harvard Yard at center left and the Cambridge Common at center right, across Massachusetts Avenue. In the foreground at extreme lower left is the sloping roof of Gund Hall, which houses the Graduate School of Design. Cathedral-like Memorial Hall is across Quincy Street from Gund Hall, and toward the right are the terraced Science Building and the Harvard Law School.

Radcliffe College Quadrangle

In the foreground is the Radcliffe College quadrangle, and the Radcliffe Observatory is in the center background. The quadrangle includes coeducational housing for Harvard and Radcliffe undergraduates.

Radcliffe College Yard (right)

The large, white-columned building (at roughly one o'clock in this photograph) is the Agassiz House (1904). Alexander Wadsworth Longfellow, Jr., a nephew of the poet, was its architect. At three o'clock is the Radcliffe Gymnasium (1898), facing Mason Street. McKim, Mead and White were the architects. At five o'clock is the Fay House (1807), the administrative building of the college. At about twelve o'clock, adjacent to the Agassiz House, is the Arthur and Elizabeth Schlesinger Library on the History of Women in America (1908), which was designed by Walter Thatcher Winslow and Henry Forbes Bigelow. It also houses the Mary Ingraham Bunting Institute on its third and fourth floors. At ten o'clock is Buckingham House (1821).

Now an independent corporation within Harvard University, Radcliffe College was founded in 1879 "to furnish instruction and the opportunity of collegiate life to women and to promote their higher education."

83

The Charles River at Dawn

Harvard houses (dormitories) overlook the river on the north (left) side. At right is a portion of the Harvard Graduate School of Business Administration.

Rowing on the Charles on a Fall Afternoon (right)

Longfellow House

At 105 Brattle Street, west of the Harvard campus, is the Vassall-Craigie-Longfellow House (1759), one of seven handsome mansions along the street owned in the 1770s by gentry loyal to the king of England. They thus earned the name "Tory Row." When the patriots occupied Cambridge in 1775, the Loyalists' property was confiscated, and General Washington made his headquarters at 105 Brattle. Henry Wadsworth Longfellow's father-in-law later bought the house for the poet and his young bride, and they moved in in 1837.

The Charles River (right)

West of Harvard's football stadium, the Charles River makes a large bend and heads toward the southwest. At right is the boathouse of the Cambridge Boat Club. In the rear are the Harvard campus and Boston's skyline.

The Arsenal Marketplace

Farther up the Charles, at Watertown, a former arsenal has become a shopping center, the Arsenal Marketplace.

Wilson Farms (right)

Located near Lexington is Wilson Farms, a large truck farm.

Lexington

Lexington, the destination of Paul Revere and William Dawes on the morning of April 19, 1775, was the site of the first confrontation between British troops, on their way to Concord, and colonial militia. At the Lexington Green, Captain John Parker told his seventy-five Minutemen: "Stand your ground; don't fire unless fired upon, but if they mean to have a war, let it begin here."

One of Lexington's activities on Patriots' Day, now celebrated the third Monday in April, is a five-mile race sponsored by the local Lions Club. It begins at the Lexington Green, continues along Massachusetts Avenue, and then returns to finish at the Green.

Concord

At Concord, which was named after a seventeenth-century agreement—a "concord" between the settlers and the Indians—a parade highlights a series of Patriots' Day activities that begins with a ceremony at dawn (5:30 A.M.) at Minuteman National Historic Park.

Following the American Revolution, Concord became known as the home of such philosophers and literary figures as Henry David Thoreau, Ralph Waldo Emerson, Nathaniel Hawthorne, and Bronson Alcott.

The Old North Bridge

As British troops searched for colonial stores of guns and ammunition in Concord, colonial militia from neighboring towns assembled west of the Concord River. They confronted the Redcoats at the Old North Bridge, forcing them back toward Concord and along the Battle Road to Lexington and Boston. At the end of the day the British had suffered 273 casualties to 95 for the Americans. Now, every Patriots' Day, Minutemen and militia meet at the re-created Old North Bridge in an annual parade past the statue of the Minuteman by Daniel Chester French.

PART FIVE

To Cape Cod and
Along the Shore to Cape Ann

Walden Pond

South of Concord is Walden Pond, where Henry David Thoreau lived for two years in a small cabin and wrote *Walden*. The land on which Thoreau built his cabin, which he moved into on July 4, 1845, was owned by Ralph Waldo Emerson, whose heirs donated it to Middlesex County in 1922. The county later transferred it to the Commonwealth of Massachusetts, which now maintains it as Walden Pond State Reservation.

Codman House (right)

Near Lincoln, south of Concord, is the Codman House, owned by the same family for over two hundred years. Built by the Russell family between 1735 and 1741, the house was originally a two-story Georgian mansion. In 1790 John Codman, a relative, doubled the size of the house "in a conscious effort to imitate an English country seat." Charles Bulfinch is said to have designed the additions.

For more than two hundred years the house was used primarily as a summer residence. Later family members made further changes in it and added a formal Italian garden. In 1968 Dorothy Codman bequeathed Codman House, also known as the Grange, to the Society for the Preservation of New England Antiquities.

Wellesley College

About seventeen miles west of Boston, on the shores of Lake Waban, is Wellesley College, a liberal-arts college for women, with a campus enrollment of 2,242. It was founded in 1870 by Henry Fowle Durant. The Galen Stone Tower, with a thirty-bell carillon, is part of the administrative building at left center. Pendleton Hall, in the foreground, follows the curve of Central Street, part of the route of the Boston Marathon. Just to the right of Pendleton Hall is the Jewett Arts Center, housing the Wellesley College Museum and the music and art departments. Tower Court, a dormitory complex, is at right. Across the lake to the rear of the campus is the white mansion of the Hunnewell estate.

Franklin Park (right)

At the southern end of Olmsted's Emerald Necklace, in West Roxbury, is Franklin Park, which spreads over more than five hundred acres and is the largest park in Boston's public park system. Considered one of the finest of Olmsted's designs for "the enjoyment of rural scenery," it is also the home of the Franklin Park Zoo.

Boston College

Boston College was founded in the South End in 1863, two years after the Jesuit Order built the Church of the Immaculate Conception on Harrison Avenue. In 1913 the campus was moved to the suburbs, along Commonwealth Avenue and Beacon Street (at right) in Newton. Gasson Hall, the original building, is the H-shaped Gothic building with a tower at lower left. Behind it is the new Thomas P. O'Neill, Jr., Library, dedicated in October, 1984. Alumni Stadium, between the campus and the Chestnut Hill Reservoir, holds 32,000. Only three home football games are played there annually, with the rest at Sullivan Stadium in Foxboro, which holds 61,000. Boston College, still Jesuit-affiliated, has an enrollment of 14,500, including graduate students, and emphasizes a solid, liberal-arts education.

Blue Hills Reservation

South of Boston, below Milton, is the Blue Hills Reservation, which includes Great Blue Hill, elevation 635 feet, the highest point on the Atlantic Seaboard south of Maine. Covering 4,857 acres, the reservation has over five hundred miles of trails, including two hundred miles of hiking footpaths and three hundred miles of marked ski trails. It has the highest downhill ski area near Boston.

Braintree Station

The southernmost stop on the Massachusetts Bay Transit Authority's Red Line is Braintree Station, south of Quincy. It includes a large parking garage for commuters who live toward Plymouth and Cape Cod, southeast of Boston. Massachusetts Highway 3, at right center, leads toward the cape.

Sullivan Stadium (right)

About twenty miles southwest of Boston, on U.S. Route 1 at Foxboro, is Sullivan Stadium, which was built in 1971 and is the home of the New England Patriots football team. Before finding a home of their own, the Patriots played at Braves Field, Fenway Park, Harvard, and Boston College.

Harvesting Cranberries (right)

Wet-harvesting cranberries on a bog near North Carver, the farmer in the foreground is using a water-reel machine, an "eggbeater," to knock the cranberries off the low-lying vines, which are flooded only at harvest time in September and October. The cranberry vines are planted over old peat swamps and then "sanded" every three or four years—covered with a layer of sand two or three inches thick. During harvest, floating berries are corralled by bog workers and carried off by conveyor to waiting trucks. About half of the entire United States cranberry harvest comes from southeastern Massachusetts.

The Kennedy Compound

Located near the center of Cape Cod's south shore, Hyannis Port is a fashionable waterfront resort where the Kennedy Compound—the Kennedy family's summer home—is located. In this photograph it overlooks the point of land at the right.

Sandy Neck Beach (right)

On Sandy Neck Beach, on Cape Cod Bay near Barnstable, boaters enjoy the isolation possible along the seven-mile-long beach, which once was much used by whalers to boil down blubber in large cauldrons.

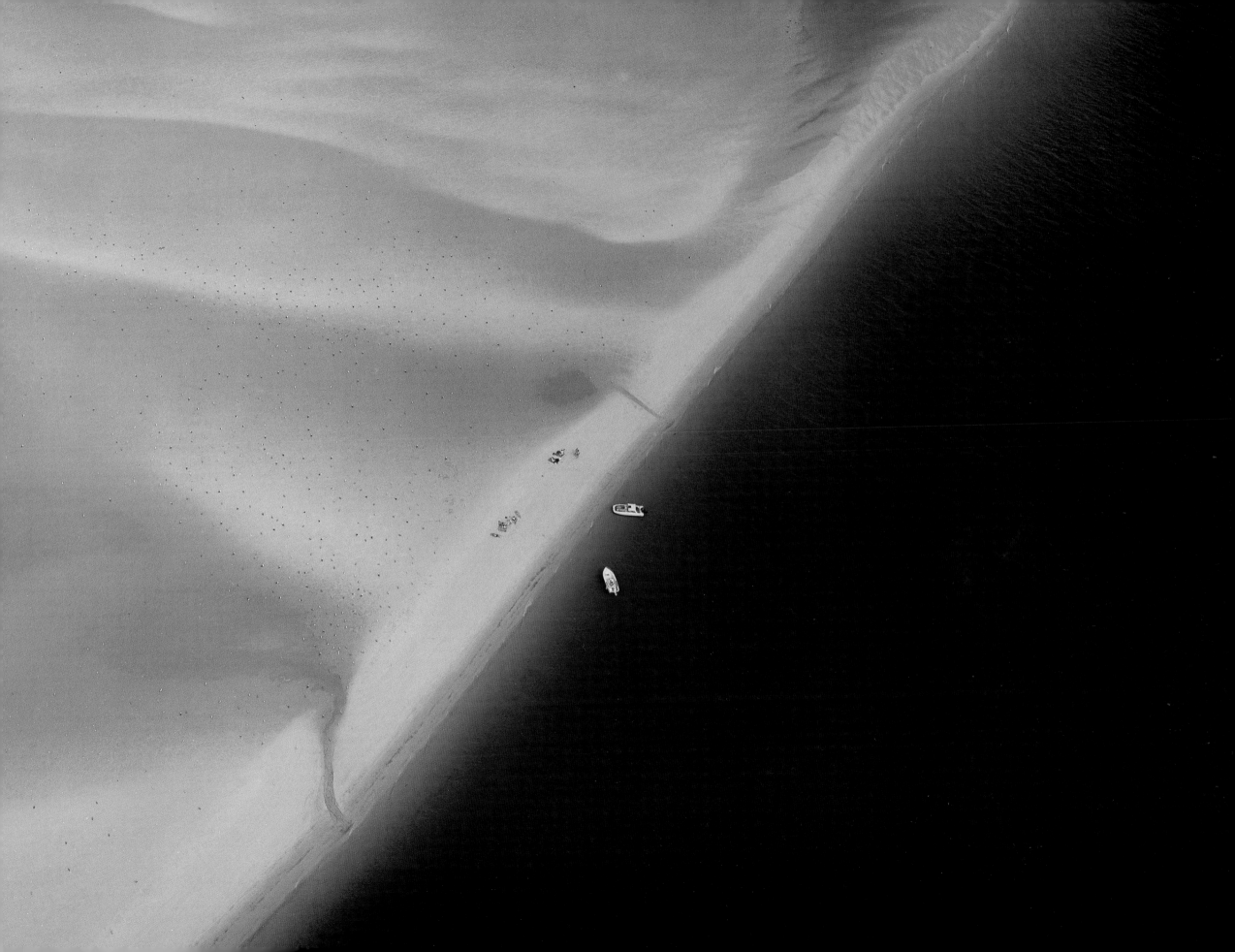

Plymouth Rock and the Mayflower II

Sheltered within a columned, templelike shrine is Plymouth Rock, a boulder at the water's edge on which the Pilgrims stepped as they first debarked from the *Mayflower* in 1620. At the state pier in the upper right is the *Mayflower II*, a full-scale reproduction, built in England (1955–1957), of the type of ship that carried the Pilgrims to the New World.

Plymouth (right)

On the Atlantic coast forty-one miles southwest of Boston is Plymouth, where the Pilgrims established the first permanent settlement in New England. The Town Brook, which enters the picture at lower left, flows through Brewster Gardens, a public park, to the sea at center right, near the area where the Pilgrims built their first homes.

At center left is Burial Hill, containing tombstones dating back to the early years of the colony. Overlooking the waterfront just above the Town Brook is a green rise called Cole's Hill, where, during their first winter, the Pilgrims buried their dead in unmarked graves to prevent the Indians from knowing how great their death toll was—it amounted to almost half the colony. Just above Cole's Hill at the water's edge are Plymouth Rock and the *Mayflower II*.

Near Cohasset Harbor (right)

A residence on its own private rock near the entrance of Cohasset Harbor

Scituate Harbor

Looking northwest toward Boston, this view shows Scituate Harbor, a favorite port of call for pleasure boaters during the summer months. At the point of land at the extreme right center is the Scituate Lighthouse (1810), deactivated over a hundred years ago but still maintained by the Scituate Historical Society.

The Adams Family Home (right)

In Quincy, birthplace of two presidents of the United States, John Adams and John Quincy Adams, is the Adams National Historic Site, home of four generations of the Adams family. The site takes in 4.77 acres of land and includes the mansion at the right, the stone library to the left of the mansion, the greenhouse to the rear, and the carriage house at the extreme right.

The house was built in the 1730s. When John and Abigail bought it in 1788, it was much smaller, with only two rooms on the ground floor and two on the second floor and smaller rooms in the attic. The cookhouse was another, smaller detached building to the rear but was joined to the main building when the Adamses moved in. The property, however, was larger then, consisting of forty acres and an orchard.

In 1946 the Adams Memorial Society gave the mansion, its furnishings, and the 4.77 acres it stands on to the American people. The site is administered by the National Park Service.

Commercial Point

On Commercial Point in Dorchester Bay, along the Southeast Expressway, Boston Gas retained a well-known local artist, Sister Corita Kent, to paint an abstract design on one of its two huge gas tanks in the early 1970s, creating a memorable local landmark. Malibu Beach in at center left, and Boston's financial district is at top center.

John F. Kennedy Library (right)

Overlooking Dorchester Bay from Columbia Point in Dorchester, the John F. Kennedy Library, designed by I. M. Pei and Partners in 1977, houses seven million pages of documents from the Kennedy years in the White House. The adjoining museum contains his desk and rocking chair from the Oval Office, and outside is his sailboat. In addition, the library contains the letters and papers of Ernest Hemingway.

Castle Island

Five successive forts on Castle Island have commanded the entrance to Boston's waterfront. Three were built by the British, the first in 1634, and the other two by the Americans, with the last, Fort Independence, constructed of Quincy granite beginning in 1801.

The stamps forced on the colonists by the Stamp Act were stored at Castle Island, which became a major British redoubt after Lexington and Concord. When the patriots mounted cannon on nearby Dorchester Heights, the British spiked their more than two hundred guns and razed the fort. In 1778 the Americans built a new fort, rededicated by President John Adams as Fort Independence in 1799.

Edgar Allan Poe served at Fort Independence in 1827, where he heard a rumor about an officer sealed alive behind a brick wall. Poe later dramatized the story in "The Cask of Amontillado."

Now no longer an island, docks on filled land handle the containerized freight at the right. South Boston is to the rear, and the central business district, off to the northwest, is at upper right.

Winthrop Beach (right)

East of the harbor and Logan Airport, Winthrop faces the Atlantic to the east and Boston to the west.

Marblehead

Seventeen miles north of Boston is Marblehead, settled in 1636, one of the major yachting centers on the east coast. On the seaward, eastward side of the harbor is Marblehead Neck, an exclusive residential area. In the foreground is Castle Rock on the Neck, with the harbor in the background.

Norman's Woe (right)

Just southwest of Gloucester Harbor, off Hesperus Avenue, which parallels the shore, is a large reef called Norman's Woe after the reef in Longfellow's "Wreck of the *Hesperus*." In the background at right center is Hammond Castle Museum.

Hammond Castle

At 80 Hesperus Avenue, near Magnolia, is a fanciful castle, complete with a drawbridge and moat, built by inventor John Hays Hammond, Jr., between 1926 and 1928. Constructed of elements from European castles and manors, Hammond's composite seeks to evoke the various castles of medieval Europe. Within the Great Hall is an organ with 8,600 pipes, many parts of which are from churches of the Continent. At the right end of the castle is a rooftop cafe.

Gloucester (right)

Gloucester, on Cape Ann about thirty-five miles north of Boston, is the oldest seaport in the nation. Still a major fishing port, it has a fleet of about 250 boats that make its harbor their home. Gloucester fishermen were immortalized by Rudyard Kipling in *Captains Courageous*.

Rockport Harbor

A little red fishing shed (center foreground) in the harbor at Rockport has been the subject of so many paintings that it has earned the name Motif No. 1. In the nineteenth century, the port's major export was granite, quarried nearby and shipped as far as South America.

Lane's Cove

A small inlet with a man-made sea wall on Cape Ann, Lane's Cove was used primarily as a granite port in the nineteenth century. The rock was shipped out on barges. The cove is still used by pleasure boaters and a few lobstermen.

Crane Beach Reservation

Beyond Cape Ann, near Ipswich, is the Crane Beach Reservation, a four-and-a-half-mile neck of land dominated by Castle Hill, which was designated a common ground by the town fathers of Ipswich in 1634. Thirty years later the land was divided among private landowners. Ultimately it was purchased by Richard T. Crane, a Chicago plumbing manufacturer who in 1925 erected a thirty-five-room Georgian mansion, designed by David Adler and landscaped by the Olmsted firm of Boston.

Following her husband's death, Mrs. Crane donated the property to the public in his memory. The Great House is annually the scene of a summer classical music series, held on the Grand Allee, which extends from the house to the cliffs overlooking the beach.

PART SIX

*The Boston Marathon
and Boston at Twilight*

The Start of the Boston Marathon

Perhaps the best-known event of Patriots' Day is the Boston Marathon, America's oldest marathon, which has been run annually since 1897 from Hopkinton to Boston, always on a Monday. The twenty-six-mile race attracts about 7,500 runners and 750,000 spectators. It takes about two hours and ten minutes for the winner to cross the finish line at the Prudential Center. Shown here is the crowd of runners at the start of the race in Hopkinton.

Runners Passing the City Hall at Wellesley, the Halfway Point

Leaving Heartbreak Hill, with Boston College in the Background

The Finish Line at Prudential Center (right)

Harvard Square

The High Spine (right)

A Note on the Photography

Photography from a helicopter presents several problems that the photographer on the ground will encounter less often or not at all: frequent haze, low contrast, continuous vibration, and shooting from a moving platform over which he may have little control. (Some photographers can fly and shoot at the same time, but for me, a professional pilot at the controls is a necessity.)

Many times I have seen a beautiful blue sky from the ground and assumed that it was a great day for aerials, but once in the air, I realized that it was not so great after all. Over most metropolitan areas there is an ever-present haze, and really clean, crisp days are rare. Such days usually occur right after a strong front has moved through, but even then there are problems. The air is clean, but it is also turbulent, making it difficult for the pilot to place the craft in exactly the ideal spot the photographer has in mind. In addition, tall buildings create their own eddies and downdrafts, and when the wind is blowing hard, the pilot has to keep his speed up for better control and fly a little higher for safety. And in Boston, it can be cold. (I prefer to shoot with the door removed.)

Sometimes we have to shoot under adverse conditions. Some events, like the Boston Marathon, will take place rain or shine, foggy or brilliant, hot or cold. If there is enough visibility to fly, we have to shoot and make the best print we can under the circumstances.

The haze also affects the color balance of the photograph. The more one is shooting into the sun, the more noticeable the haze becomes, and the bluer the picture. On the ground, this can be compensated for by adding color-correcting filters on the lens, but in the air one is constantly moving and the color balance is constantly changing. Thus, my personal preference is to shoot with color negative material, rather than transparencies, and to color-balance the prints in my own darkroom.

Because of the haze and the aerial viewpoint, there is almost always less contrast than on the ground. Consequently, I prefer Eastman Kodak's Kodacolor over their Vericolor Professional film for aerials. Both are astonishingly sharp, but Kodacolor has more contrast. In general, I use the slowest film available, but I prefer to shoot at a shutter speed of 1/1000 second to minimize the effects of vibration. Consequently, I use Kodacolor 400 whenever the light level drops. It is not as grain-free as Kodacolor 100 but is still a remarkably sharp and brilliant film. After sunset, the light level drops rapidly, and even at maximum aperture, shutter speeds will fall to 1/60, 1/30, and even 1/15 second. At about this point, the light is beautiful but fleeting, and in order to shoot just a little longer, we "push" Kodacolor 400 another couple of stops, to ISO 1600. Even with such pushing, 1/60 second is really not enough to achieve a sharp negative in a helicopter, and by the time we have had to drop to 1/15, only about one negative in ten is usable.

We make our own color prints for reproduction (Gisela O'Brien, an excellent printer, makes all my color prints). Since we are working in color negative, we have the option of using two photographic color papers, Ektacolor 74 and 78, the latter of which provides more contrast than the former. In conjunction with selective dodging and burning in (to lighten or darken specific areas of the print), we feel these two papers give us greater control of the final image than using transparency film and depending upon the color separator and the printing press to match color balances.

Vibration is always a problem, but obviously it is a greater one when the light level is low, necessitating slower shutter speeds. In the air, as on any vibrating platform, the photographer must "float" his camera almost on his fingertips, getting it away from the body and insulating it from the vibration of the aircraft. The problem is intensified by the focal length of the lens. The longer the lens, the greater the magnification of the subject and the greater possibility of loss of sharpness due to vibration.

Speaking of lenses, I used Pentax lenses from 45 mm to 300 mm with the Pentax 6 × 7 camera. The camera is sturdy, solid, and dependable, and has shutter speeds to 1/1000 second. The lenses are impeccable. For a number of views, I used the Pentax 75 mm Shift lens, which allowed a moderate, semi-wide-angle view, but without the tilting verticals that accompany a lens that does not have such built-in potential for correction.

For this project I began to use the 300 mm, f/4 telephoto. Formerly, I had a fixed opinion that the 165 mm was about the longest practical length for aerials with this format, but the 300 mm fooled me. For such a long lens, it is surprisingly handholdable, even down to some rather slow speeds at twilight, and it allowed close-up views that otherwise were out of the question because of altitude limitations. For a few extreme close-ups, I worked out of a platform suspended from the 150-foot boom of a motor crane.

Fenway Park at Game Time

INDEX